The Art of
Positive Laziness

Adriaan Diepeveen

PRE-READING WARNING

Not reading and studying the content of this book
can lead to unnecessary stress, wasted time and
energy, as well as pointless activity in the future.

CONTENTS

PREFACE

Does the following sound familiar? Work is piling up, days seem to get shorter, and we constantly seem to be busy with one thing or another without making much progress. However, when you look around, you notice that there are some people who never seem to be busy at all yet still get a lot done. You would think a day is just as long for everyone, so what are these people doing differently?

The quest to answer this question is what led me to develop a lifestyle called Positive Laziness. It is a system, a way of thinking and acting that enables you to become one of those people who never seems to be doing much yet still achieves a lot.

What can you expect from this book?

In this reading you'll be introduced to the art of

positive laziness, a way of life to achieve more with less. We will look how we can create more free time by recognizing and eliminating all the nonessential tasks. Furthermore we will take a look on how we can complete the remaining tasks in the most efficient way. Next we'll discuss ways to improve your overall effectiveness and look at some techniques to talk yourself out of useless tasks at work and school. In the final part of this book we will discuss how Positive Laziness can help you to achieve your life goals and dreams and why these big dreams are so important.

This book is written to help you to create order in the busyness and chaos of daily life, and helps you create more free time. 'Do less, achieve more' is the main theme of this book. I tried to keep it as short and essential as possible. I hope you enjoy the read.

PART 1: SETTING THE RECORD STRAIGHT

Since this book is all about the positive side of laziness, the logical thing to do is to start with the following question: 'What is laziness?' Laziness has had a bad reputation for centuries now. At one point in time the church even went so far as labeling laziness (in the form of sloth) as one of the Seven Deadly Sins! So what is it? And what gives it its bad name? It's time to set some records straight.

We will start by exploring and busting three major myths about laziness and success:

1. Laziness is an inherently bad thing
2. Laziness keeps you from being successful
3. Laziness and self-discipline cancel each other out

After that we will quickly look at why being busy all the time, by being overwhelmed with tasks and working hard to get through them, is actually a form of negative laziness.

Myth 1: Laziness is always a bad thing

The idea that laziness is a bad thing comes forth from misinterpretation and abuse of the term laziness itself. When we think of a lazy person, the picture that quickly comes to mind is one of a profiteer; someone who refuses to do anything and makes other people do all the work. However, laziness does not always have to be a bad thing. In a lot of cases it is actually a good thing. There is a good reason why we are born with lazy impulses. Before looking why this is, let's start with defining what laziness precisely is.

Laziness is: The absence of the will and energy to undertake a certain action. It is nothing more or less. Laziness is a built-in firewall which protects us from blindly rushing into pointless tasks and prevents us from wasting time and energy. However, since we are brought up with the notion that laziness is a negative character trait and should be avoided altogether, this mechanism is deteriorating. We are being trained to suppress the impulses of laziness, not knowing that by doing so we are switching off our natural defensive mechanism which protects us from distress and burn-outs.

In the meanwhile we are showing signs of laziness without realizing it. This is because society does not recognize these phenomena as manifestations of laziness. One example of these phenomena is being too busy to get anything done. How this is actually a manifestation of laziness we will discuss later on. First let us shine a light on the yin and yang of laziness.

The two sides of laziness

Laziness itself is a neutral thing, laziness can be good or a bad depending on the context. Even though this book is all about the positive manifestation of laziness, we will take a quick look at the dark side of it. To be able to use laziness to our advantage, we first have to be able to tell when laziness is good or bad.

Negative Laziness

Negative laziness is the manifestation of laziness which gives laziness its bad name. It's this form of laziness which leads to piled up work, missed deadlines and a shortage of healthy exercise.

Negative Laziness can be easily recognized by the following standards: Laziness is bad when it leads to harm to you, your work, your friends and family or your environment. It all depends on the effects of not doing certain things.

We will now take closer look at a few examples of Negative Laziness, starting with one of the most dangerous forms.

Mental Laziness

Mental laziness is one of the most dangerous forms of negative laziness. Mental laziness comes down to being too lazy to think for oneself. It's accepting and copying ideas and stereotypes without ever thinking them through. It's doing things in a certain way just because everyone else is. It's accepting that certain things are true just because everyone else believes it, without checking the facts properly.

People who exhibit this kind of laziness are an easy target for manipulation. People that don't think critically are easy to influence, for better or worse, because they won't doubt the presented facts properly. Making sure you are not one of those people being controlled by others is easy; just use your brains where you got them for. Avoid mental laziness at all costs.

A small example

The following short story shows how people unconsciously copy behavior without ever doubting how useful certain habits are. It also illustrates the way to counter this mindlessness.

Mike walks into the kitchen where his sister is preparing a piece of meat. Just before she puts it into the oven she takes a knife and cuts it in two. Mike asks his sister why she cuts the meat in two before putting it in the oven. "I don't know, that's how mom always does it" she replies. Mike doesn't give up and decides to ask his mom why she always cuts the meat in two before putting it into the oven. His mom replies to his question "I don't know that's how your grandmother used to do it". Mike decides to settle this once and for all and he calls his grandmother. "Grandmother, why did you always cut the meat in two before you put it into the oven?" Mike asks over the phone. His grandmother bursts into laughter and answers "Because I used to have a really small oven, it was the only way it fitted."

In the previous story you could clearly see how both Mike's sister and mother showed signs of mental laziness. Be like Mike and stay critical. Check the facts if possible, and ask yourself if the things you do are really the best way to achieve something. The fact that everyone is doing something a certain way doesn't automatically make it the best way to do it. Keeping this in the back of your mind is crucial while practicing the art of positive laziness which consists of looking for alternative ways to achieve the same goal with a lot less effort. It's self-evident that mental laziness stands in the way of positive laziness.

Giving up

Another manifestation of negative laziness is giving up. Here I don't mean giving up on doing something when you suddenly realized that it was pointless. By all means, as soon as you realize something is going nowhere, please stop immediately. However, giving up because you are too lazy to look for solutions when you are facing obstacles is clearly a form of negative laziness.

A lack of ambition

A lack of ambition is a manifestation of negative laziness which is inclining towards mental laziness. A lack of ambition springs forth from a fatalistic worldview. The view that things just are the way they are, and that you don't have any control over it. By this people convince themselves that, because there is nothing they can change about their situation, there is no use in trying it. This is how it becomes a self-fulfilling prophesy. It's the attitude that makes people give up before even trying. It's what people gets to give up their dreams and prevents them from ever achieving their goals and reaching their full potential. This is a truly tragic thing. Beware of this destructive attitude. The best way to ensure something won't succeed is by just not trying it at all.

In the last part of this book we will continue on the topic of ambition. For now we will move on to exploring ways in which laziness is used as an excuse to cover up for something else (and by that giving laziness a bad name).

Laziness as an excuse

Next to a lot of people not knowing the difference between positive and negative laziness there is another reason why laziness has such a bad name. Often when we say we are too lazy to do something, we actually mean that we are just too scared. While blaming laziness for avoiding a certain action, the actual cause can be found in the (unconscious) fear of the consequences. No matter if these consequences are positive or negative.

It's easier to say that you are too lazy to find another job or to start your own company than to admit that you are afraid of taking the leap. Laziness is being used to camouflage a lack of courage. Fear of change, fear of the unknown and a loss of certainty. People who say they are too lazy to start the journey towards a better life are usually just too scared to take the first step.

Fear can have a big influence on people, especially the fear of loss; the loss of certainty, friends, respect, credibility, love, or money. Just name it. People who are being paralyzed by their fear might seem to exhibit laziness because it stops them from taking certain actions. This doesn't mean it really is laziness. Learn to see the difference.

Sometimes we are so scared of the potential outcome of certain actions that we'd rather don't do anything at all. This because we are scared of what other people might think or say about us. We live within the constraints that we put on ourselves. We are afraid of letting other people know how we really feel, afraid to say out loud what we really think, afraid to take new paths and try out new ways to achieve our goals. We often do this without realizing how dumb this is. We are keeping ourselves small. By this we are our biggest obstacle in achieving our life goals. The only thing standing in the way of success is our own fear. This doesn't have to stay this way. The thing a lot of people fail to see is that there are two kinds of fear.

One the one hand there is natural fear and on the other there is learned fear. Natural fear is the kind of fear that makes us avoid potentially deadly situations like jumping off the top of high buildings. It keeps us from doing the dumb stuff like putting our hands in the mouths of sharks and makes us run away in time when we encounter a tiger in the jungle.

Learned fear on the other hand constitutes of most social phobias like being afraid of rejection, as well as the fear of speaking in public. While natural fear revolves around protecting our lives, learned fear revolves around protecting our ego. Most of these learned fears are unfounded and can be discarded. That's why it's important to train yourself to distinguish the two forms from one another. When fear is of the natural kind you'd better listen to it. Learned fear however, might be better ignored or conquered.

The problem with learned fear is that a lot of the time it feels very real. It can be pretty nerve wrecking to give a speech in front of a hundred people. However, there is nothing that really can go wrong. In the worst case scenario you might forget your lines or screw up a few words. Unless you are performing for some Mafia boss who can't stand slipups, there is no real life threatening danger involved. The world won't end if you screw up the presentation.

A weird thing about a lot of social fears is that the fear of the consequences increases the chance of those consequences really occurring. For example, by being afraid that you will forget your lines at a big presentation, the fear itself will probably be the cause of you forgetting your lines. It is a vicious circle. Luckily, by conquering your fears, you'll be able to decrease the chances of failing.

Conquering (learned) fear

Conquering fear takes nothing more than temporarily putting your emotions on stand-by and letting your rational mind take over again for a minute. Ask yourself what the worst case scenario could be, how likely this is to happen, and if that would really be the end of the world. In case of learned fear, action beats fear. It's about just getting over it and taking the first step. As soon as you do it you'll realize it wasn't as bad as you'd expected. You need to get over this hurdle by stepping it up and just going for it. The more often you do this the easier it gets. Start with small challenges and work your way up from there.

Myth 2: Laziness keeps you from being successful

This myth has its roots in the still widely popular misconception that hard work is the key to success. Today there are still people who seem to believe that if you just work really hard you will end up being successful. Alas, the world doesn't operate that way. Not hard, but effective work is what leads to results. The people who work the hardest (physically) are usually not the ones who are paid the most, while people who work with their head are being paid a lot better.

If hard work really was the key to success then everyone who worked hard should be successful while the persons who refrain from hard work could never become successful. Alas, there are a lot of hard working people who still have to work around the clock just to get by.

For example imagine a factory owner and his employees. Who is more successful? The owner who delegates all the actual work and takes in all the profits or the employee who works day in day out as hard as he can just to get by? Of course the definition of success can vary for different people but it should be clear that just hard work is not the key to success.

If you want to achieve something, it is not about working hard but about working effectively. In the end it is the result that counts, not how hard and long you worked for it. Positive laziness helps you to be more result oriented and helps you to achieve your goals while spending less energy.

Remember: It's not about how hard you work, what counts is how much you achieve.

Laziness does not keep you from being successful. As a matter of fact, positive laziness helps you to become more successful by pushing you to find more effective ways to achieve your goals.

Myth 3: Laziness and Self-Discipline cancel each other out

This myth fits the idea that laziness is a negative thing. While a lot of forms of negative laziness can be contested by improving your self-discipline, self-discipline and laziness do not have to cancel each other out.

The common idea is that someone is either disciplined or lazy. A combination of these two extremes may be hard to imagine but it's still possible. Positive laziness makes sure you won't do any unnecessary tasks while in the meanwhile self-discipline helps you to get the remaining essential tasks done as fast as possible. More about self-discipline can be found in part 3.

Even though a lot of forms of negative laziness can be contested with self-discipline, self-discipline and laziness can still complement each other. You can be proactively lazy where you flat out refuse to do anything that doesn't bring you closer to your goals but do those things that do bring you closer consistently in a disciplined way.

Why being too busy is a form of negative laziness

Often you hear people complaining about how busy they are. They got so much to do and complain about not having enough time to get anything done. These people always seem to keep themselves busy. They constantly seem to be doing one thing or another without getting any closer to their goals. Even though these people might be hard workers they display a form of negative laziness.

"What?! You must be kidding me", you might think. "How can being flooded with tasks and working hard trying to get them done be a form of negative laziness?" Well, the answer is pretty simple. Being too busy is the result of being too lazy to take the time to review your to-do list and think it through properly. It's being too lazy to set priorities. Paradoxically this leads to extra work and wasted time and energy. Not doing one thing leads to doing a lot of other things.

Being too busy is usually the result of one or more of the following causes:

- Not setting priorities
- Being unable to see how useful a task really is
- Bad planning
- Mindlessly rushing into tasks
- Not being able to say no

On top of that, being busy is quite a good excuse to avoid the tasks that really need to be done but you dread doing. An excuse, being too busy is actually nothing more than that. It's being too lazy to stop for a second and ask yourself if that what you are doing really is a useful way to spend your time and energy. Being too lazy to review your to-do lists, set priorities, and focus on doing the things that really matter the most.

PART 2: THE FOUNDATIONS OF POSITIVE LAZINESS

In this part we will take a look at the three main elements of the art of positive laziness. They are: Elimination, searching for more effective and efficient ways to achieve certain tasks, and relaxation. These elements are essential for a life full of positive laziness. Applying these elements ensures that you won't do more than really necessary, helps you to get those essential tasks done faster, and enables you to go through life more relaxed. However, before we start looking at these elements one by one, I would like to take the time to give The Art of Positive Laziness a worthy introduction.

The essence of positive laziness

Positive laziness is a way of life. It's a way of thinking and acting that focuses on the things that really matter the most, the essentials in life. It's about continuously looking for more effective ways to achieve your goals. This lifestyle enables you to see through the illusion of seemingly important tasks and helps you to recognize and eliminate pointless tasks more easily. Positive laziness can also be referred to as intelligent or smart laziness because it is mainly a way of thinking. Instead of blindly rushing into tasks, you first take the time to ask yourself if those tasks are really that necessary. With the tasks you have to do anyway, you look for alternative ways to get them done with less effort and in less time.

At the first glance Positive laziness can look like quite a lot of work for something that's called positive laziness. However, the better you get at applying the principles of the art of positive laziness, the easier it gets. Once you've mastered the art it will become a natural way of going through life.

Mindset

The Art of Positive Laziness is mainly a way of thinking. Since every conscious action flows out of a thought it's not that surprising. To counter pointless actions you will have to tackle the problem at the core.

It is not only about banning out pointless tasks, it also aims at removing distress from your life to help you to get a clear mind and be more focused.

3 Elements of Positive Laziness

There are three elements at the heart of positive

laziness. By using these elements as guidelines you can easily determine if laziness is indeed positive. Laziness is positive if:

1. It makes you avoid pointless work
2. It gets you to search for more effective and efficient ways to achieve a goal
3. It makes you avoid or reduce distress and fatigue

Eliminating (tasks, not people)

Elimination is the element of Positive Laziness that has the biggest time and energy saving potential. It is the art of setting priorities. Even though we're not always aware of it, we usually spend a lot of time doing things that don't really matter at all. These seemingly important tasks keep us from achieving our real goals and are big time and energy wasters. To make sure we don't waste anymore of our valuable time and energy, it is crucial to teach ourselves how to systematically recognize and eliminate these pointless activities. To find out if the task you are about to start at is useful you can ask yourself the following three questions:

1.   What are the consequences of not doing this task?

     When neglecting the task at hand has no serious consequences for you or others (meaning it is not negative laziness), it is safe to skip the task altogether.

2. Does completing this task bring me closer to my goals?

> If not, the task is a waste of time, you could have spent the time better at tasks that do get you closer to your goals.

3. If this was the only thing I would get done today, would I be satisfied?

> This question helps you to figure out how high on your priority list the task should be.

These are the three questions that are the base of the art of elimination. Even though these questions seem simple, in practice a lot of people seem to have difficulties with answering the second one. Does completing this task bring me closer to my goals? This question however is *the* question which prevents us from being overworked and too busy.

Goals

The main reason why so many people find it difficult to answer the second question (does this task bring me closer to my goals) is because most people don't have a clear vision of what they really want to achieve. When you don't know where you would like to arrive, it is hard to figure out the shortest route to that destination. Without knowing what your goals are, it is impossible to figure out if the task at hand brings you closer towards them or leads you away from them.

Probably no one likes to spend his or her time and energy on meaningless tasks, but what is the definition of a meaningless task? A meaningless task is nothing more than a task that does not serve a desirable goal. This is exactly why it is so important to set clear goals. Goals help you to give meaning to your actions.

Big vs. Small goals

Having clear goals helps you to see which things really matter and helps you to determine which tasks are crucial and which are not. Sadly, most people don't have a clear picture of what they really want.

Even though having clear life goals helps enormously with putting positive laziness into practice, you won't have to worry about those just yet. If you haven't determined which big life goals you want to chase you can start practicing the art of elimination on smaller goals. By smaller goals I mean things like meeting deadlines at work, short term company targets, and getting through school, as well as other things that you come across on a daily basis. With big goals I mean the life goals, your biggest dreams. For more about these dreams, see part 5.

Aim vs. goal

While determining if doing a task serves a clear purpose, it is important to be able to tell the difference between the aim and the goal of the task. For example: When you are writing a job application letter, the aim is to provide a clear overview of your skills and qualities so you give your future employer a good impression of you. The real goal of writing the letter however, is to get accepted for the function you are applying for. When doing homework for school, you are supposed to follow the assignment so you will master the teaching material. However, following the assignments (the aim) is not always necessary to master the material (the goal).

It is important to see the difference to make sure you won't attach to much value to certain tasks. Make sure the tasks don't overshadow the goal. Focusing too much on the way can make you lose sight of the destination. Whatever you do, make sure you know what you are doing it for or don't do it at all.

Orders from above

When you can't seem to find out the goal behind a task that you have to do at work or at school, you can always ask your boss/teacher about the reason for letting you do it. Don't be satisfied with an answer that shows any resemblance with 'because I say so'. Keep asking until you have a clear answer. Answering 'because I say so' is the same as saying that they don't know the answer either. If your boss/ teacher can't answer the question of what's the goal behind a task, tactically ask if you could skip the task altogether since it's clearly distracting you from the work that really is important. The funny thing about this situation is that you are reversing the roles. Instead of you having to justify why you didn't do a certain task, now your boss/ teacher has to justify why he or she is bothering you with pointless work and distracting you from the more important stuff.

Elimination exercise

We will now take a look at a short exercise in removing the non-essentials. Take for this exercise an empty piece of paper and a pen, and follow the following four steps:

Step 1: Take the empty paper before you and write down all the things you still have to do. As soon as you have done this, ask yourself for every item the three crucial questions: What are the consequences of not doing this task? Does completing this task bring me closer to my goals? And, if this was the only thing I would get done today, would I be satisfied? Use these questions to determine which tasks are really important and cross off the rest of the tasks.

Step 2: For the remaining tasks, try to find the underlying goals of those tasks and write them down. Cross off all the tasks for which you can't find a clear goal. The only exception is when not doing the task would be negative laziness.

Step 3: Take a good look at your remaining list and pay attention to the underlying goals of the tasks. Just because a task has an underlying goal, doesn't always mean that that goal is worth the effort. Finally cross of all the tasks for which the goal is just not really worth the trouble of doing the tasks.

Step 4: Take another clean piece of paper (or use the

back of the first) and rewrite your final to-do list. Again, write down the underlying goal of the tasks. This helps you to motivate yourself to actually do those tasks. It also helps you with finding more effective ways to achieve your goals. How this works will be discussed in the next section on finding more effective and efficient ways to complete tasks and achieve your goals.

Looking for more efficient ways to complete your tasks and achieve your goals

In this section we will take a look at effectiveness and efficiency, especially the difference between the two concepts. It is not just about completing tasks in a more efficient way, it is about becoming a more effective person as well. In the previous section you already made a list of things to do and then trimmed it down to the essentials. Now we will figure out how we can complete the remaining tasks on that list as fast as possible, as good as possible and with the minimal amount of effort.

Effectiveness vs. Efficiency

Effectiveness and efficiency are two terms you often hear in one sentence, this is because they are more or less connected. At the same time this is exactly the reason why these two terms are often being mixed up. A lot of people still find it difficult to separate the two. To make sure that at least you won't ever mix those two concepts up we will look at both of them separately and then compare the two.

Efficiency

Efficiency is purely about the way you perform a certain act. Completing a task in the most efficient way is nothing more than performing the task as economical as possible. In other words, it means completing a task with minimal effort, time and costs. How efficient a task is performed has nothing to do with the underlying purpose or goal of the task. Efficiency is all about the task itself.

Effectiveness

Effectiveness is all about the goal that you are trying to achieve by completing a certain task. It's about the effect that is caused by the performing of the task. How effective a task is entirely depends on the goal you are trying to achieve. If the task gets you closer to achieving that goal it is effective. If not, it is a waste of time and the task is ineffective. It's no rocket science. It's as simple as that.

It is almost impossible to work effectively without being efficient. On the other hand, it is amazingly easy to work super-efficient without being even a bit effective. You can spend your whole day doing tasks in a highly efficient way without getting a single step closer to your goals, or even getting your daily tasks done.

A few examples of these tasks that you can easily do very efficiently without being effective are:

- Carrying an empty suitcase up and down the stairs a million times.
- Counting the average number of drops of coffee that fall from the coffee machine after you've filled your cup.
- Customizing your toothbrush by painting miniature flames on it.
- Walking the dog leash (without the dog).
- Flossing your pet otter.
- Counting the pieces of toilet paper.
- Checking if the length of a roll of tape is indeed as long as the package says it is by measuring it yourself.
- Braiding the fur of your bunny.

You can do the previously mentioned tasks as efficient as possible. However if they don't get you closer towards your goals they are not very effective. This is why it is important to start with making sure a task is effective before looking for a way to complete it as efficient as possible.

The underlying goal

In the previous exercise you've been asked to write down the underlying goals of each task. The reason for this is that it helps you become more effective. What you should want to do is to strive to achieve those goals as fast and properly as possible. With this underlying goal in the back of your mind it also becomes easier to see if a task really is important.

Multiple layered goals

Before you can find the most effective way to achieve something you first need to clearly define what it is you are really after. Without doing this, focusing your effort to find more efficient ways to do your tasks might even work counterproductive.

The first thing you should ask yourself before starting at a task is if it's the most effective way to achieve the underlying goal. This might require you to look a little deeper into that goal than you'd normally do.

For example: If you are doing some cleaning at work, finding a more efficient way to clean the place so you can go home earlier might work counterproductive if you get paid by the hour. Especially if you clean for a living and the real underlying purpose is to make the money so you can pay the rent. Once you realize this you can either decide to look for a higher paid job or start offering cleaning services as a freelancer where you get paid per cleaning session instead of per hour. In this case you employing more efficient cleaning methods will enable you to get to your desirable endpoint more effectively (making the money to pay the rent in less time).

Another example; imagine that calling your colleague to make an appointment that he picks you up to go to a company meeting is on your to-do list. The underlying goal of calling your colleague is of course getting him to pick you up to get to the meeting. However, the underlying goal of the meeting itself could be deciding on a new marketing plan. Even though calling your colleague may be the best way to get him to pick you up and arrive at the meeting, the deeper underlying goal, the deciding on a new marketing plan, might be better achieved by holding a digital meeting. This would be a lot more effective and efficient because now, no one has to drive all the way to the central meeting point so a lot of time is saved. Fuel costs and CO_2 emissions are avoided as well. So with this deeper underlying goal in mind it might be a better to, instead of calling your colleague, send one e-mail to the whole team in which you suggest an e-meeting.

In the previous examples you could see that there can be diffcrent levels of underlying goals. So, underlying goals can have underlying goals. Like getting picked up to be at the meeting is the underlying goal of calling your colleague, the deciding on the new marketing plan is the underlying goal of being at that meeting. Always keep your eye on the deeper underlying goal. Try to look further than just the superficial one.

Finding other roads

Now you know the deeper goal of the tasks at hand it is time to find the most effective and efficient way to achieve that goal. Keep in mind that there are multiple ways to get where you want to be, and not every way is the shortest one. You already have the advantage of knowing the deeper underling goal which reduces the chance of you getting distracted by nonsensical tasks. The thing you really need to do is achieve the goal, not necessarily take the steps you would normally take.

Keep it simple

When finding out the fastest way to achieve the underlying goal it's important to keep the following two guidelines in mind:

Guideline 1: The less steps, the better. Minimize the amount of steps you have to take to achieve the goal to the absolute necessary amount.

Guideline 2: Keep it simple. Keep your plan of action as clear and simple as possible. Know what you are doing. The simpler the plan, the less detours it has. Look for the shortest and easiest way to achieve the goal.

Learn from others

Yes, it is self-evident that you should always learn from your own mistakes and successes. However, often it is even more effective to learn from how others have achieved comparable goals. By this you are levering the experience of other people who got it by putting their time and energy into it, without having to do the same. You are saving yourself time and energy by tapping into the experience of others. The good thing about this is that you are not hurting others by doing this. They have already put in the time and effort in collecting the knowledge and experience on how to achieve those goals. That time won't come back anyway. It is only logical to take advantage of it.

How much time and energy you can save by doing this can clearly be seen by what you can learn from books. In a single book which you can read in just a few hours, you can sometimes find the results of years of searching for the right solution. The lessons the writer has learned from years of trial and error you can take in by just reading it. Without having to make all the same mistakes yourself.

Learning from mistakes vs. learning from successes

Of course it is ideal to learn from the mistakes of others so you won't have to make the same ones. It can be a good move to look for people who made a lot of mistakes while trying to achieve the same goals as you. However, it is far more interesting and effective to look for people who found the solution for the problem you're facing (finding the most effective way to achieve your goal).

A short illustration: Thomas Edison invented a proper working light bulb after more than 10.000 attempts (the details of the exact number vary depending on the source; the point is that it took a lot of tries). When you would like to make a light bulb yourself, you could study the 9.999 failed experiments so you know what doesn't work. However, it would be a lot smarter to just look at the one experiment that did work. Do not just search for mistakes you can learn from, focus your search on the successful solutions found by others. Learn from success.

The same applies to your own experience of course. It is self-evident that you should learn from your mistakes to assure that you won't repeat the same ones, but try to focus more on your successes. Sadly, we are not always as conscious of our own successes. This is for a large part because we tend to only mark big achievements as success. To put that straight I will share a short definition of success.

Success is nothing else than achieving a goal you've set for yourself. No matter how big or small that goal is. This means you are successful every single day in a way. We tend not to notice this because we put too much emphasis on our mistakes.

Count your successes

Did you plan on getting out of bed today and did this? Congratulations! That's a success. Did you plan on reading this book? Again, congratulations! Did you plan on taking a walk and did it, hooray another success. Realize when you succeed at things and learn from it. Make mental notes on what went right. This focus on success has the benefit of boosting your confidence by helping you to place failure into perspective. Instead of dwelling on it endlessly when you make a mistake in whatever you're doing, realize that there are countless more successes to counter that one little error.

Relaxation

The art of relaxation comes forth from the third guideline of positive laziness: Laziness is good when it makes you avoid distress and fatigue. It is especially the 'hard work leads to success' myth that causes us to pointlessly deplete our energy reserves. It's the thought that we have so much to do, and not enough time to do it all that drives us to rush into tasks blindly. In effect, the list of things to do seems never ending.

By applying the art of elimination, you put an end to this by cutting your to-do list down to the absolute essentials. By doing so you will achieve more in less time which in turn gives you more time to chase your higher life goals. However, be careful that you don't fill up all your newfound free time with other tasks, even if they are useful. Your body and mind need their rest.

By making sure you get enough rest you will give your body and mind the chance to recover energy and strength which enables you to work more effectively. A well-rested healthy body and mind are a lot more productive than those on the verge of a burn-out. Burn-outs and fatigue are phenomena which are often caused by our obsession with hard work. Positive laziness helps you to avoid these pitfalls.

Distress

When you are constantly pushing yourself, stressing yourself to the max, your body eventually can't stand up to the pressure anymore. Long-term exposure to an overload of distress impairs your immune system, which makes you more susceptive to diseases. Worrying too much makes you irritable and moody, which impairs your ability to think rationally and clearly. Not only is hard work not the key to success, it's unhealthy as well when it's not balanced by enough rest.

Take it easy

To keep your body and mind healthy it's important to get enough rest. The first tip on how to go through life more relaxed is to stop hurrying. When you think you are running late, missing a deadline or are too busy, it only makes you more stressed. This leads to a clouded mind, which makes you more likely to not pay enough attention, resulting in making mistakes. Time seems to speed up as well as soon as we get into a mental hurrying state.

Stop hurrying altogether. Leave a few minutes earlier from home if you need to be somewhere in time. Get up a little earlier to take your time and enjoy a relaxed breakfast. Take the time for the things you need to do. You can't be too busy anyhow, so just focus on the task at hand. Just take one step at a time. Think about how you are going to perform a task before you start, and more importantly, ask yourself if you should be doing that task at all. Think before you act. And don't forget to take a good breather once in a while.

We will now look briefly at a few tips on physical and mental rest.

Physical rest

- Make sure you get enough sleep at night. Find out which amount of sleep works best for you since the optimal amount of hours varies from person to person. Sleeping too long is tiring as well, so get up in time.
- Take powernaps to refresh yourself. Take one cup of coffee and then lie down and shut your eyes for about 15 minutes. After these 15 minutes the caffeine kicks in as well. Make sure you don't get into a too deep sleep (get up after the 15 minutes). When you shut off completely it will take at least 30 minutes before you are fully awake again.
- Get enough exercise. Exercising helps you to feel fitter and more energized.

Mental rest

- Stop hurrying, take your time.
- Meditate once in a while.
- Take a relaxed walk in the fresh air from time to time.
- Try staring at the stars at a clear night sky for half an hour.
- Don't worry about matters that you can't influence, you're not planning on changing, are none of your business or have nothing to do with your goals.

In part four we will look deeper into the subject of a peace of mind.

PART 3: ACTION, GETTING THINGS DONE

No matter which goals you are trying to achieve, with tasks you should always take following three steps:

1. Judge if the task is useful. (If not, stop here.)
2. Find out the most effective and efficient way to get the task done.
3. Complete the task.

It's important to take all three steps. Forgetting step one is a case of mental laziness which creates the risk of starting at pointless tasks. Forgetting step two means risking wasting valuable time and energy while doing a task. Forgetting step three is negative laziness as well, which results in you not going anywhere because nothing gets done.

Action

When you have determined which tasks really need to be done, you know the underlying goal, and have found the best way to achieve it, it is time for the last step: Really doing and completing the task. In this part we will look at how positive laziness and self-discipline are connected. We will look at how you can motivate yourself to get started at the tasks at hand and see why it is best to get over them as quickly as possible.

Self-discipline and positive laziness

Like mentioned briefly earlier on, a lot of forms of negative laziness can be countered with self-discipline. Think of exercising to keep yourself fit, keeping up with your homework, and making deadlines. Self-discipline is what enables you to do those things.

In this section we will focus on how self-discipline and positive laziness complement each other. We will start by briefly shining some light on self-discipline itself before looking at how we can increase it. Finally we will look at how self-discipline fits into a lifestyle full of positive laziness.

What is self-discipline?

Self-discipline, everyone has it. Some of us have a lot of it, some only have a little, but what is it exactly? Self-discipline is the ability to get yourself to perform tasks regardless of your emotional state and without anyone else having to motivate you. It's the art of self-motivation.

To be able to go through life independently, self-discipline is a crucial. Without self-discipline it would be impossible to stand upon your own two feet because it would mean that you'd be totally dependent on others to get you to do stuff. Getting up in the morning, brushing your teeth, eating and even going to the bathroom all demand a certain amount of self-discipline. It's a good thing that everyone has at least a little of it.

Why is it so important?

Why would you bother to increase your self-discipline? Increasing your self-discipline helps you to become a more energetic person and makes it easier to achieve your goals. It also gives you more control over your life. To get back to the three steps given at the beginning of this chapter, to go through step three you need self-discipline. The more you have of it, the easier it is to take the step.

How to increase your self-discipline

Increasing your self-discipline helps you to become a more effective person, but how do you increase it? Or in other words, how do you get yourself to do the tasks that really need to be done? As mentioned before, self-discipline is the art of self-motivation. One of the reasons why we can't get ourselves to start at certain tasks is that we just can't seem to find the energy to do so because we don't see the point in it.

By eliminating all pointless tasks we have already tackled this problem. All the tasks that remain either bring you closer towards your desired goals or not doing them would inflict harm on yourself or others.

Increasing your self-discipline is quite easy; it's mainly just about doing it. It's a switch of mentality. Instead of constantly procrastinating tasks, and thinking of weak excuses why you can't do something, you just do it. You don't have any legitimate excuses left because all tasks left after the elimination process serve a clear purpose. Not doing those tasks would either harm your surroundings or keeps you from achieving your desired goals.

Self-discipline works like a muscle, the more you rely on it, the stronger it becomes. At the other hand, not using it weakens it; just like the strength in your muscles decreases after you haven't exercised in a long time. The more often you just do what you have to do, the easier it gets to do the same the next time. Increasing your self-discipline is all about just doing what you set yourself to do. Important to keep in mind is that you have to be consistent. By consistently just doing the things you set out to do, without coming up with excuses or postponing it endlessly, it becomes a habit, a part of who you are. With this you become more reliable as well since you can depend on yourself to do what you say you'll do.

Procrastination

A lack of self-discipline doesn't always result in not doing certain tasks. Often it leads to procrastination of the tasks, by which a lot of time is wasted. Not only is time being wasted because it takes longer to achieve your goals, procrastinating tasks also acts as an energy vampire. Worrying about all the things you still have to do sucks up energy and leads to dreading the tasks even more. Here your mind often plays dirty tricks on you, the longer you evade a task, the more work it will seem. In the end it looks like a much bigger task than it really is.

Attitude

Increasing your self-discipline and tackling procrastination is all about a change of mentality. When you dread doing a task it might be a wise thing to ask yourself why this is. If the answer turns out to be about you being scared of the potential result of the action then ask yourself if the fear is founded. When you can't see the point in doing the task, see if you can just eliminate the task.

Procrastinating is a form of negative laziness which wastes precious time. To rebel against this, the key thing you need to change is your attitude. Realize that the tasks you are doing are useful, and that the faster you get them done the faster you get rid of them and the faster you achieve your desired goals. Once the task is completed you'll never have to worry about it again.

Deadlines

Make sure you don't set deadlines too far ahead in the future. A task or project tends to take as much time as you set for it. For example, if you need to turn in a paper next week, the chances are that you'll probably finish that paper a day before the deadline. If you had to turn in the same paper tomorrow, you'd probably have finished it just in time as well. This is why you should set deadlines as early as possible for yourself. In the event that something unexpected comes up you at least have some extra time to deal with it. Sticking to these self-imposed deadlines requires self-discipline and is right away a good way to strengthen it.

Try living according to the motto: Don't wait until tomorrow with that which could be done right now. The tasks that survive the elimination process have to be done eventually anyway.

A clean slate

In the previous chapter you've been asked to put together a to-do list. After that you've been asked to filter out all the pointless tasks. What remains should be a list of all the things that you would have to do eventually anyway. We will shortly look at getting rid of this to-do list (not by throwing it out the window or setting it in flames, but by getting the tasks done) so you can continue with a clean slate. It is easier to get yourself to do tasks when you know that you don't have piles of work still waiting for you when you finish. This is because you know that as soon as you're done, you are really done. Once your slate is clean again you can easily take the time to look if tasks really are useful. And if that's the case get over it soon, so you will have genuine free time on your hands again. But before it's that far let's get rid of the tasks cluttering up your list now.

Starting with a clean slate is easily realized by taking four simple steps. The first two steps you have already taken in the previous chapter. Should the unthinkable happen and you are drowning in work again, take this page before you again and take all four steps. These steps are:

Step 1: Get ready

Take a piece of paper and write down all the tasks you still have to do, the task that have to be done today, as well as the tasks that will have to be done in the near future. Since you have already done this in the previous chapter you can skip this step at the moment.

Step 2: Eliminate

Take a critical look at your to-do list and figure out which tasks can be deleted from the list. Use these 3 questions to guide you:

- What are the consequences of not doing this task?
- Does completing this task bring me closer to my goals?
- If this was the only thing I would get done today, would I be satisfied?

Use these questions to find out which tasks can be safely removed from the list (note: removing tasks from the list, just because you don't feel like doing them is NOT positive laziness). After this, write down the underlying goal of the task and judge if that task is the most effective way to achieve that goal. This step you have already taken in the previous chapter so you can skip this one for the moment as well.

Step 3: Organize

Take a look at the remaining tasks and write down when the tasks have to be finished (hint: tasks that should have been done already have a high priority, write down today behind these tasks). Then rewrite your task list in the order that the tasks have to be finished. Write the tasks that have to be done today on top, followed by those that have to be finished tomorrow etcetera. See the example.

To do:

Task - underlying goal - deadline
Homework, learn economic model, tomorrow
Clean my room, be able to find everything and save time, the day after tomorrow
English essay, improve my average grade, next week

Step 4: Start right away

As soon as you have completed your final to-do list it is time to get to work. Finish the tasks in the order of priority in the most efficient manner. This is the point which will test your self-discipline. Keep in mind that the faster you complete the tasks, the sooner you get rid of them. The remaining tasks on your list have to be done eventually anyway so the faster you get over it, the better.

Make sure you complete the entire list, even the tasks that need to be done in a week or so. As soon as you are done with it you can start with an entirely clean slate and you'll have genuine free time on your hands. When you still have tasks to be done, even if it's not immediately, your mind won't be able to completely relax. You'll still have the notion in the back of your mind that there are still tasks waiting. Starting with a completely clean slate again does wonders for your mental health.

PS: Just focus on one task at a time and finish that one task as fast and good as possible before starting with the next one.

Self-restraint

Before we end this chapter I would like to address the matter of self-restrain. Unlike self-discipline which is about doing things, self-restraint is all about the opposite. Self-restraint helps you to consciously keep yourself from doing things. To be able to work effective and efficient you need to develop both.

Self-restraint vs. Self-discipline

Self-restraint and self-discipline look like each other's counter-poles since they both aim at achieving the complete opposite. To do, or not to do. Even though they are each other's opposites, they are still very compatible. Combining both is crucial if you want to effectively achieve your goals.

For example: When you want to improve your physical fitness you need self-discipline to get yourself to exercise. At the same time you need self-restraint to help you refrain from unhealthy habits like excessive drinking or smoking. When you want to lose weight and you are sticking to a diet, again you need both self-discipline and self-restraint. At the one hand you have your self-discipline which makes you eat at the right times and makes sure you get the right healthy food from the supermarket. In the meanwhile, self-restraint keeps you from eating the unhealthy snacks.

Combined self-discipline and self-restraint enable you to take full control of your own life. To practice the art of positive laziness you need both as well. Self-restraint helps you to refrain from doing the useless tasks while self-discipline helps you to get over the remaining tasks as quickly as possible. Luckily, increasing your self-restraint is not that complicated. We will end this chapter with a small exercise.

How to increase your Self-restraint

Step 1: Choose your favorite snack

If possible choose something that doesn't have to be kept warm or frozen, and preferably something with a large amount of units like a bag of crisps. If you're a chocolate addict like me, choose a bag of chocolate peanuts of break a chocolate bar into small pieces.

Step 2: Place the snack strategically

Put the crisps, pieces of chocolate, or whatever other snack you chose on a small plate and place it in your sight. Make sure that while you are busy with other things, or when you are just relaxing, the snacks are clearly visible.

Step 3: Take one

Take one unit of the chosen snack, for example one chocolate peanut. Just one! This is to get the hang of the taste and make the juices in your mouth start to flow, increasing your craving. Leave the rest of the snacks in front of you and keep your hands off it.

Step 4: Take one every 5 minutes

Take just one unit every 5 minutes. Keep yourself from taking more than one, this is the training. As soon as you get better at it increase the time span to 10 or more minutes.

With the previous exercise you can put your self-restraint to the test. The more you practice, the easier it gets. You can combine the exercise with clearing your to-do list. Instead of taking one unit every five minutes, you can take one unit every time you finish a task.

PART 4: PRACTICAL APPLICATIONS

This part is all about the practical applications of positive laziness. It is written to quickly skim through from time to time to get some ideas when time seems to be scarcer than it should. We will look at the 80/20 principle, go through some ways to keep a clear mind, see how you can improve your reading speed, discuss some ways to implement the art of laziness at school and end with some other practical applications.

The 80/20 principle

There is quite some literature to be found that discusses the 80/20 principle, some books are even entirely dedicated to it like "The 80/20 principle" by Richard Koch. Even though this is not one of those books dedicated to the principle, a short explanation of this principle can't be left out in a book about effectiveness, efficiency, and time saving.

In short the 80/20 principle comes down to this: 80% of the results come forth from 20% of the input. For example:

- 20% of the customers are responsible for 80% of a company's revenues
- 80% of all the wealth is owned by just 20% of the population
- 80% of the time you hang out with friends you spend with 20% of your friends
- 20% of your clothes you wear 80% of the time
- 80% of the time you only use 20% of your stuff

The list can easily continue for a while but you probably get the idea. Find out which 20% of your efforts are responsible for 80% of the desired results and focus your time and energy on those activities. Find out what you do different in this 20% of the time and learn from that. Now we know about the 80/20 principle we can continue with the practical applications of positive laziness, starting with how you can realize a calmer and clearer mind.

Peace of mind

A clear mind enables you to go through life more focused. Keeping your emotions under control helps you to let rationality prevail so that you can make the right decisions at the moments it matters the most. Worrying too much clogs up your mind, at the expense of your ability to think clearly and of your effectiveness. It makes you more likely to make the wrong decisions. A neat tidy mind is a clear mind. To find out which thoughts get in the way of a clear mind we will take a look at what we are unnecessarily worrying about.

Things you shouldn't worry about

The following list consists of things which can drive us crazy from time to time while not helping us one bit. The following you can safely neglect worrying about:

Things you can't influence

Worrying about things you can't influence only drains your energy. If you can't change something because it's outside your realm of influence, you should forget about it and direct your focus to something else. No matter whether you worry about it or not, nothing will change as a result. You might as well save your mental bandwidth and attention for things you can influence.

Things you're not planning to do anything about

If you are not going to do something about the thing that is bothering you, you should let it rest. If you're not going to change it anyway, why pay attention to it anymore? Either do something about it or let it go.

Stuff that's none of your business

There is nothing wrong with some empathy, but keep out of matters that are none of your business. Focus your energy on yourself before getting into other people's business, especially when you can't influence it anyhow.

Events that have already past or are still to come

When things have past, you can't change it anymore so let it rest. When you are stressed and nervous about having to give a presentation or visiting the dentist, realize that you can't do much about it now anyway. Besides, it still lies in the future while you live in the now. When you are anxious about having to speak in public in front of 300 people, realize you are not giving the presentation right now.

Why worry about stuff that still has to happen? Just focus your attention to the present moment. If you get all queasy about the idea of having to take place in the dentist chair, remind yourself you are not there at this moment. Relax, experience the now. You don't have to worry about any of it at the moment since it is not happening now. Besides, a lot of time the things we look up to end up not being as bad as we thought they would be.

Things that have nothing to do with your personal goals

Know which things really matter. Focus on the things that are relevant for achieving your goals and realizing your dreams. Don't let yourself get distracted by the things that only keep you from achieving them. Never lose sight of your goals and dreams. Keep in mind which things really matter the most for you and just focus that.

What others think about you

Finally, don't worry too much about what other people think about you. Too many people waste their energy and time because they do that which they think other people expect them to do, instead of setting and chasing their own goals. Most people don't think that much about you anyway. Often they are far too busy with their own daily worries. Don't too pay much attention to negative criticism either. Don't let yourself be talked out of ideas by just one person. Keep in mind that there are around 7 billion people in the world. Who is this one person to tell you that something is impossible? There's a big chance that millions of people have a different opinion about the matter. Just believe in yourself.

Try to put things into perspective and don't pay too much attention to the negative comments of others. Sadly, there are people in this world that like to talk other people down so they can feel better about themselves. Don't let these people mess with your head, who do these people think they are? This might sound a little egocentric but you got to remember that you are the most important person in your life. After all, it is your life, and it's your responsibility to get the most out of it. Other people have their own lives to influence. Just ignore the people who only express negative criticism.

How to become a more effective person

What follows is an overview of some tips on how to become a more effective person that are quite obvious. However, that these tips are quite obvious doesn't necessarily mean that they are already being followed. It's not knowledge, but applied knowledge that is power.

Do something with your ideas

Everybody has great ideas from time to time; few of these ideas are actually being implemented. Most of the ideas you come up with will never come back, so make sure you write them down. Make sure you always carry some kind of notebook with you to write down your ideas as you come up with them. These can pop up in the most unexpected moments, so be prepared. As soon as you come up with a great idea, do something with it. Having a great idea which is not implemented is just as good as having no idea at all.

Action speaks louder than words

This advice is an extension of the previous one. There is a big chance you know someone who has been walking around for years with the idea to start his own company, go on a trip around the world or write a book. This person usually tells everyone about it. However, at the same time nothing ever really happens, and the person keeps walking around with the idea.

Don't waste your time by telling everyone about the things you still want to undertake someday, just start realizing those plans instead. Don't talk about doing stuff, but actually do it. There is nothing wrong with telling people about what you are working on, but make sure you actually get started in the meanwhile.

Focus on just one task at a time

Even though multi-tasking is being praised at a large scale as the solution to becoming more effective and efficient it is still a better idea to keep your focus on just one task at a time. By this you can concentrate more easily at the task at hand and you won't be distracted so easily. By concentrating more you'll be less prone to making mistakes. This prevents you from having to do things twice. Just focus on the task at hand and finish it as fast and good as possible before moving on to the next. By this I don't suggest that if you still have to return a book to the library, want to see how late the movie in the cinema starts and have to get some bread from the baker, you shouldn't do this in one trip to the city. Whatever you can combine you shouldn't shy away from, as long as you still can focus on each task separately.

Effective communication

We spend a lot of time communicating; being able to communicate effectively saves you a lot of time and frustration. We will take a look at some guidelines on getting your message across efficiently and go through some tips to either avoid or get you out of pointless conversations and arguments.

Keeping an eye on the goal

To communicate more effective it's crucial to keep your eye on the goal of the interaction. By doing this you'll be able to keep control of the subject and it helps you steer the conversations back on the right track when it wanders off.

Get to the point

Avoid small talk. Don't ask empty questions which you don't expect an answer to. When you call someone to find out how late a meeting is, don't ask questions like 'how are you?' and talk about the weather unless the weather might have any influence on the timing of the meeting you are calling about. Keep it short and just ask how late the meeting starts. By this you'll prevent wasting your time and that of the person you are calling.

Speak clearly

Pay attention to your articulation. If people are struggling to understand what you are trying to say, chances are they won't get much of the message you're trying to get across.

Be alert

Pay attention and remember what has been said. Avoid having to ask things twice because you weren't paying attention for a second. Keep your full attention at the conversation at hand. This means really being present. Put your phone away for a moment when talking to someone face to face.

Ask to clarify

To avoid any misunderstandings it is important to clear away any potential misinterpretations. You could do this by formulating the point of view of the other in your own words and ask if this is indeed what he/she was trying to say. This practice is also called active listening and can be used for resolving conflicts as well by forcing the opposing parties to put themselves in the shoes of the opponent. In this case the next person may only bring forth his or her next point after formulating the other party's point of view in such a way that he or she agrees with it.

Arguments and other pointless conversations

Sometimes we just can't seem to escape it and we get stuck in pointless discussions and arguments. This is usually just a huge waste of time and energy and gets us nowhere. Fortunately there are some simple methods to avoid these stressful time wasting discussions, starting by recognizing them in an early stage.

What's the point?

Before engaging in any argument or discussion, ask yourself what the point of it is. If taking part in the discussion doesn't get you any closer towards achieving your goals, it's often better to let it slip even if the other party is clearly wrong. Just walk away from it. The best way to get the most out of an argument is to avoid it altogether.

There's no use in winning every time

Don't try to out-argue the other every time, even when you are right. Some people are just less sensitive to rationality and well founded arguments. Don't waste your time trying to get others to see you are right to people who aren't listening anyway. In some cases it might be best to end the conversation by saying: 'I get your point.' Or in the worst case scenario even by saying 'you're probably right'. Excuse yourself and get on with more useful things, or at least things that are less stressful.

It's better to acknowledge that the other person is right (even if he/she isn't) than to get stuck in a pointless and endless discussion. When the outcome of the discussion doesn't affect you it doesn't matter whether you win or lose the argument anyway.

Learn how to distinguish meaningful information from pointless data. When a discussion is going nowhere and the other side is only bombarding you with unfounded shaky arguments you know that it's time to end the discussion.

Take a deep breath

Things that unconsciously slip off the tongue at the wrong time while not paying much attention can get you into a lot of trouble. In some cases it might even lead to endless further discussions you'll need in order to talk yourself out of it and apologize. This happens more often than we realize because we spend a lot of time operating in autopilot-mode. When we aren't alert we just react to stimulus in the way our brain has programmed itself. Sometimes this leads us to say stupid things without realizing it, things that could trigger some angry reactions.

To avoid getting yourself into discussions in which you have to talk yourself out of things you said while not paying attention, the only thing you have to do is to be more conscious about your own answers. From now on, take a deep breath and think about what you are about to say before you speak. When someone asks you a question, don't respond right away. Take a breath, let the question get through properly, and answer afterwards. In this few seconds you can right away determine if the conversation is going anywhere. This enables you to steer it in into a meaningful direction if not, or end the conversation altogether.

Don't worry that people might think that you are being slow when you pause for a moment before you answer a question. It only shows that you take the question seriously and you're not just sprouting random answers. This helps you to leave a more intelligent impression and enables you to make a more meaningful contribution to the conversation. By answering more focused and thoughtfully you'll be able to get to the point faster.

Vague questions

A vague question leads to a vague answer. Only ask clear and focused questions even if this requires you to put a bit more thought into it. When someone is asking you a vague question ask this person to clarify the question. Never answer a vague question. Without knowing what you want to know you'll never get the right answer. When you don't know what someone is trying to ask, you can be as creative as you want in answering, but it's just guessing.

How to talk yourself out of useless tasks

As soon as you realize that you're wasting a lot of precious time and energy because of tasks you've been ordered to do (by your boss or teacher for example) it is crucial to be able to talk yourself out of those tasks. Note that this only works if those tasks really are pointless. You can use the following method to talk yourself out of these pointless tasks:

Step 1: Reason

> Appeal to the common sense of your boss/teacher. Show him with clear and founded arguments why a certain task only distracts you from more important matters.

Step 2: Suggest an alternative

> When you try to get out of having to do a task

that you think isn't the most effective way to achieve the underlying goal, suggest a better alternative. Show that you are not just trying to get away with doing nothing at all, but in fact are being highly efficient with your time. Show that you know what you are doing.

Step 3: Propose a trial

When proposing a new way of doing things to achieve the underlying goals a lot faster you shouldn't be too surprised if your teacher/ boss is skeptical at first. Propose a trial so you can prove that it works. Present it as something that can be turned back if it doesn't work as promised. This way, your teacher/ boss keeps the impression that he or she is still in full control, and you save yourself a lot of work. It's a win-win situation.

Positive laziness for students

Since positive laziness is indispensable at school, we will now take look at some tips on how to go through school in a more effective way. This helps you to get through school more easily. When I started applying positive laziness I noticed that school got a lot easier over time. On top of that, eventually I had more time left then I could fill. Talk about a luxury problem.

Pay attention in class

By just participating actively in class you'll save yourself a lot of time. Since you have to spend those hours at school anyway, you might as well try to make the most of it. Paying a little bit of attention in class can make the difference between pulling an all-nighter and getting some decent sleep the day before a big test. Don't hesitate to ask questions when you don't quite get things or if the lessons are going too fast for you. Everything you absorb during the lessons you don't have to learn at home anymore. All the homework you finish at school can't rob you of your free time once you get home.

Increase your neuroplasticity

Neuroplasticity is the ability to make new connections between your brain cells. It's about how fast you can absorb new information and how well it sticks. The bigger your neuroplasticity the less time and effort it takes to learn new stuff. Humor has a positive effect on this. Watch some funny video's for about half an hour on Youtube before starting to go through the teaching materials. Not only helps this to relax, it makes you absorb the material faster as well.

The essence of the materials

Make sure you have an overview of all the teaching material which will be asked about in the next test as quick as possible. Knowing the study goal helps you to judge which homework assignments are essential and which can be skipped. Only do the assignments which bring you closer to achieving that learning target.

Specific questions

Information is better retained if it is an answer to a question you really want an answer to. By converting the learning target into specific questions you'll be able to get to the core of the teaching material faster and remember it better. Start with the question: What do I want (or in the case of school, what do I have to) know? Think of questions that help you achieve the goal of getting to know it.

For example, imagine you have a history test on the 16th century of Holland. You need to be able to tell something about how the trade of goods was done in that time, the politics, and some major events that took place in that century. For this you could formulate the following questions:

- What where the most important elements of trading in the 16th century?
- How was the country governed?
- What were the most important events of that time?

Once you formulated the questions it's all about finding the answers to them and you will have covered the essence of the materials. I know this might seem too simple to work, but it really does. Make sure you know what you want to know, find the answer and you're done. Follow the KISS (keep it simple stupid) principle. Don't complicate the matter.

Speed-reading

We will now look at some ways to increase your

reading speed. There are two ways to do so. The first is to physically increase your reading speed, as in more words per minute. The second one is all about reading efficiently by skimming through the text. We will start by looking at this method first.

Efficient reading

Efficient reading is about only picking up the most important parts instead of reading the full text. This method is perfect for getting the essence out of textbooks while studying.

Tip 1: Determine you reading purpose

Before you start reading, determine your reading goal, there are two main types of reading goals:

- Finding the answer to a specific question
- Picking up the core of the text

Tip 2: Don't read the words out loud in your head

Just let your eyes sweep across the page instead of reading every word out loud in your head.

Tip 3: Start by reading the question before looking at the text

Exercise: Finding the answer to a specific question

Read the following italic text from Wikipedia (http://en.wikipedia.org/wiki/Cloud) and answer the following question: How high is the reflectance of deep and dense clouds?

Cloud

A cloud is a visible mass of droplets of water or frozen crystals suspended in the atmosphere above the surface of the Earth or another planetary body. A cloud is also a visible mass attracted by gravity, such as masses of material in space called interstellar clouds and nebulae. Clouds are studied in the nephology or cloud physics branch of meteorology. On Earth the condensing substance is typically water vapor, which forms small droplets or ice crystals, typically 0.01 mm (0.00039 in) in diameter. When surrounded by billions of other droplets or crystals they become visible as clouds. Dense deep clouds exhibit a high reflectance (70% to 95%) throughout the visible range of wavelengths. They thus appear white, at least from the top. Cloud droplets tend to scatter light efficiently, so that the intensity of the solar radiation decreases with depth into the gases, hence the gray or even sometimes dark appearance at the cloud base. Thin clouds may appear to have acquired the color of their environment or background and clouds illuminated by non-white light, such as during sunrise or sunset, may appear colored accordingly. Clouds look darker in the near-infrared because water absorbs solar radiation at those wavelengths.

If you did it correctly you didn't start reading it

immediately. You would have skimmed through the text until you spotted the words 'dense deep clouds', and read the part until '70% to 95%'. After that you would have stopped reading it altogether and went on reading the normal text.

Getting to the core of the text

To be able to quickly make proper summaries it's crucial to be able to get to the core of the text. To do this quickly you should follow the following guidelines:

1. Take a look at the whole

    Read the headings, look at the pictures and read the first and last sentence of each paragraph.

2. Ask questions

    Wonder who, what, where, when and why.

3. Pay attention to bold, italic and other words that stand out from the text

Increasing your physical reading speed

Increasing your physical reading speed is all about practice. It helps to keep in mind that reading is nothing more than capturing and processing images. While reading, our eyes tend to skip back and forth between sentences and words. Using a pen or your finger to guide your eyes through the text helps you to avoid this. This saves time you otherwise would spend on reading things twice.

Another exercise you can use while trying to increase your reading speed is to read 5 pages really fast. Continue (or go back 5 pages) by reading in a more relaxed pace. When you read the 5 pages 8 times faster than normal and after that cut back to reading at a speed 3 times faster than normal, reading 3 times faster doesn't feel that fast anymore.

Other positive laziness stuff

We will end this chapter with some short summaries/ overviews concerning positive laziness.

Questions for practitioners of the art of positive laziness

Here's a short list of questions which should cross your mind on a daily basis as a practitioner of the art of positive laziness.

* What's the purpose of this task?
* Is the underlying goal worth the effort?
* Does completing this task bring me closer to achieving my goals?
* Can't I just skip the task?
* How would I normally do this?
* Is there another, more efficient way to achieve the same goal?

Pointless tasks and actions

Refrain yourself from the following:

* Tasks you do because you assume that other people feel like you should do them.
* Starting at things you deep down know you won't finish.
* Continue with things of which you realized by now that they are pointless, just because you've already started.
* Starting at tasks where the underlying goal is unclear. Not knowing what you are doing.
* Trying to win a discussion when the end result doesn't matter anyway.
* Trying to answer vague questions.

Keep in mind

* First eliminate before looking for efficient ways.
* Think before you act.
* Just because something takes a lot of time and effort doesn't make it meaningful or important.
* 'I'm not lazy; I'm just a highly effective person' (an excuse to use when you are dealing with people who don't get the point of positive laziness.)
* An impossible task is nothing more than one that's insufficiently defined.
* It doesn't matter how hard you work, what counts is how much you achieve.

The art of laziness' main principle:

Only that do which is absolutely necessary, but do

this as quick and good as possible.

PART 5: POSITIVE LAZINESS AND LIFE GOALS

The importance of dreams

Previously we have looked at how goals give meaning to tasks. The same applies to life as life goals and dreams make our life more meaningful. A meaningful life = A life with a purpose, a goal. Striving towards achieving these goals gives us something to live for, and pushes us to get the most out of ourselves. This keeps us growing and prevents us from getting stuck at the level we are now. Our life goals, our dreams, give us a reason to get up in the morning and to get moving. Chasing our dreams helps us to give direction to our life. At the same time, picturing ourselves realizing those dreams fills us with energy.

Think Big

Don't set your life goals too low. There is a good

reason for this. Goals that are set too low don't have the same ability to inspire you as the bigger ones. If the bar is set too low, achieving the goal doesn't provide any challenge. By this you can't get really energized much by the idea of achieving it. Goals that are completely achievable for you at this moment don't encourage you to push yourself, while big goals push us to grow.

When setting your life goals, don't think too much about your present situation. Instead, think about the situation you want to be in. Don't let yourself be constrained by your present knowledge or skills. Nothing is impossible as long as you figure out the right way to do it and stick with it long enough. Skills you are missing or are lacking can be trained and the missing needed knowledge can be learned.

For example: Say you want to become a rock-star but at the present moment you can't even play a single note on a guitar yet. Go learn how to play it. Your potential is only limited by your own mind. Believe in yourself and allow yourself to dream big.

Why big goals are easier to accomplish than smaller ones

A funny paradox is that in practice, big goals are easier to achieve than mediocre ones. This is because only a few people really dare to dream big and believe enough in themselves. This causes the large majority to set 'realistic' goals, mediocre 'easily' achievable goals. This causes the competition to be a lot greater when actually trying to achieve it. For example, it is easier to start up your own company and find the right personnel than to find the 'perfect' job. This is because a lot more people are looking for a fun and decent job than people that have the guts to start companies.

Big dreams are less likely to be lost out of sight than smaller ones at times that things don't go as planned. This is because the goal is always bigger than the obstacles that get in the way. Picture it as a giant mountain on the horizon. Even behind a large forest the top still is clearly visible. Would you have chosen a smaller goal, say a little house at the foot of the mountain, there only had to be one big rock in the way and you would have lost sight of it.

Knowing where you want to go

Having sky-high goals serves as a guide in your life. They function as an always visible landmark to keep you on the right track, the path towards the life of your dreams, a future that you create. But how do you find your ultimate goal in life?

About hobbies and work

There are people who say that as soon as you made a job out of your hobby it isn't a hobby anymore. They recommend to leave your hobbies for what they are, your leisure time activities. These are the same people advising you to keep your hobbies and work strictly separated. Personally I couldn't disagree more with these people. As soon as you turn your hobby into your job, it isn't a job anymore.

Why wouldn't you spend your days doing the things you are passionate about, when you can make a living out of it on top of that? Why would you want to spend your days at a job you don't like to only spend time on your passions in those scarce free hours, when you could spend your whole days doing that which makes your heart beat?

Dreams

Your ultimate life goal is nothing else than fulfilling your dreams. Realizing the, in your opinion, perfect life. To figure out how your ultimate dream life looks like, you could start with the following thought-experiments:

Your perfect day

Imagine how your perfect day(s) would look like, assuming that everything is possible. How would you spend your days if you had total control? If you had everything you wanted to have, and could do whatever you'd like to. Where would you spend that day, and with whom? What would you like to do all day? (You don't have to narrow yourself down to just one perfect day, if you're like me you'll probably have more than one idea about how a perfect day would be.)

Your perfect life

Now that you have a picture of how your perfect day would look like, it's time to start thinking about how you want your life to be like in five years. Where do you live, how do you make a living? And more importantly, how well does your vision about your perfect day fit into that life? Just let your imagination go wild, remember that everything is possible. The only limiting factor is the reach of your imagination.

You can never live a greater life than you can imagine. If you can't picture yourself winning an Olympic medal you can forget about it. Not because it is impossible, but because you don't believe in it yourself. No matter if you think that you can or can't do something, you're always right. Use this to your advantage. Believe in yourself and dare to dream big.

Setting the right goals

How do you know that you are setting the right life goals? It's pretty simple actually: You will know you are chasing the right dream if the thought of fulfilling it fills your soul with energy and makes you feel fully alive. The dream you're chasing is the right one if it inspires you. Properly set goals motivate you to get the best out of yourself. When you have something that gets you out of bed every morning, all filled up with energy, and you can't wait to get started, you know you are on the right track.

From thought to paper

As soon as you have a clear picture of your ultimate goal, it's time to transform the idea in an actual plan. Start by writing (or typing if you are afraid you won't be able to read your own handwriting after a year or so, this even happens to the professionals) down what your dream is. Just by writing down the dream you already made the first step towards realizing it. Be as specific as possible in describing what you want to achieve. If you have more than one life dream write them down separately.

Be clear

Make sure the goals you set are as clear as glass. Becoming rich, for example, is a way too vague goal. If you want to become rich, determine how much money you want to have at the bank and when you want to have it there.

Become a famous sport-star is also a too vaguely set goal. Write down in which sport you want to be famous, and for what. If you want to become an international champion in a sport, determine which championship you want to win. Without a clear goal in mind it is hard to determine when you've actually achieved it. Be as clear as possible.

Planning

Now you have determined and wrote down your life goal(s) it is time to find out how to achieve them. Fortunately you got a supercomputer at your disposal to help you with laying out the way towards this destination. This supercomputer is your brain. We've all been blessed with a wonderful machine that is built to solve problems, like figuring out a way to make the impossible possible. It's crucial to know how to take advantage of this.

When you re-read the life goals you wrote down and think it is impossible, the thinking stops right there. Should you, on the other hand, look at your goals and ask yourself 'how can I achieve this?' You will start the whole solving progress. Search and you will find. Asking is nothing more than searching for the answer. Ask and you will find the answers.

When confronting yourself with questions you really want to know the answer to your subconscious mind will look for that answer. Your subconscious is a master in finding the answers to these kinds of questions because it has access to all the information you ever took in during your life, even though you can't remember that information consciously anymore. Trust your intuition; it's nothing more than your subconscious mind working for you.

We will now look at some ways to get your mind started. We'll start with a small thought experiment.

Steps back

Since large goals aren't achieved overnight and they might seem a bit intimidating, it is wise to break them up in smaller steps. One way to do this is by the 'steps back' method.

Picture the ultimate goal in your mind. Now, imagine the milestone that comes just before that. For example, if we take the rock-star dream. The step just before achieving the last one might be being broadcasted on TV and the radio. The step before that might be a big successful concert, and the step before that could be winning a national talent show. Continue to take steps back until you reach the point where you are now. When you've done that, the only thing left is to write these steps down in the reversed order you just thought of them and you got yourself a plan.

Once you have the plan written down it is time to apply positive laziness. See which of the steps you could eliminate without jeopardizing the end result. Then think of the most efficient way to take the steps that remain. Again use the KISS principle. Don't make things any more complicated as strictly necessary. The simpler the plan is the better.

Ask for advice

Should it ever happen that you really can't figure out how to achieve a certain goal, there is always something called advice. You can always ask for advice from those people who already achieved a comparable goal. You can learn a lot from the persons who went before you. Should it happen that in the history of mankind no one ever achieved something comparable to the goal you are aiming at, you could always turn to your friends. Ask them if they want to help you brainstorming. The more people take part, the more good ideas you can come up with.

Achieving your goals

Now you have determined what your goals are, and

which step you have to take to achieve them it is time for the final step, achieving those goals. We will see how we do this by starting to look at some ingredients of a successful life.

Prioritize

Make priorities and don't be afraid to eliminate tasks. Always apply the methods of the art of positive laziness with your life goals in the back of your mind. These are the ultimate underlying goals of all your actions. Make sure you don't waste so much time on trivial matters that you never achieve your goals.

Self-discipline

Skip as much tasks as possible, but do the remaining tasks immediately. Train your self-discipline on a daily basis. You don't have any excuse to stall or not perform the tasks that bring you closer to your ultimate life goals. The longer you wait with taking those steps, the longer you'll have to wait to realize those dreams. Don't make yourself wait. Your dream life is already in sight. The only thing left is just taking the steps towards it, and that's something that only you can do.

Perseverance

Don't be taken out of the game by the obstacles you might face on your path. Know what you are striving for and conquer the obstacles. The reason why so few people get the most out of their life is because most people don't have enough faith in themselves, not because they are unable to.

Don't pay much attention to the doomsayers that try to talk you out of your plans by saying you're unable to realize them. Often this behavior is just a reflection their personal lack of confidence. When someone is trying to convince you that you can't do something, use this as a motivation. Prove that they are wrong by accomplishing it anyway.

A formula for success

We talked about the definition of success earlier in this book. We will briefly look into it a little closer. This is as well a summary of the materials discussed in this chapter so far.

Step 1: Choose your goal

Know where you want to go. Set clear and challenging goals. If goals are too big to achieve at once, break them down into smaller steps.

Step 2: Keep your goal in sight

Don't lose sight of your dreams. Never stop asking yourself if the things you undertake bring you closer towards realizing those dreams or are just distracting you from them. Keep moving towards them until you realize them.

Step 3: Achieve the goal

This last step is all about taking the right steps. Just go

for it. It's that simple. Whoever said things should be complicated to work properly anyway?

The success formula above is applicable every time. No matter how big or small the goal is. The only difference is that with the really big goals you sometimes need to break those up into smaller steps. This doesn't change the principle behind it. You can apply the same formula to these smaller steps.

Finally

This concludes this short book on the art of positive laziness. Apply the methods discussed in this book on a daily base and you'll be amazed by the time you'll save and how fast you'll achieve your goals. Not applying the principles of positive laziness is just foolish. Why would you refrain from looking for the most effective and efficient ways to achieve your goals? Why would you worry about trivial matters? And, why would you waste time and effort doing pointless tasks? And is it such a weird thing to give yourself a chance to get enough rest?

From here on it's all up to you what you do with the information. Just keep in mind that not knowledge but applied knowledge is power. To benefit from the information, you have to start using it.

The only thing left to say is the following: Thanks for reading this book. I wish you all the luck and I hope you'll live a relaxed effective life full of positive laziness. And don't forget to tell your friends about it.

Thanks again!

Adriaan Diepeveen

ABOUT THE AUTHOR

Adriaan Diepeveen was born in the Netherlands in 1990. He studied Innovative Business Services in Finland. Currently he's back in the Netherlands designing web applications to streamline workflows for companies via his company Musebox. His free time he spends skateboarding, playing music, and writing.

To read more about positive laziness and achieving your goals visit his blog:

www.AdriaanDiepeveen.com